Florida
on my mind

GRACE DAVIES

" *Florida is a state with a 'never-never' quality that attracts, delights, and enchants.... Florida is a sanctuary, a refuge of sun and sand and sea, a fountain of youth where it is widely believed that none of us need ever grow up.* "

Jim Bacchus,
Forum

FALCON®

> *" I could see why Florida is a golden word. As I went along I found that more and more people lusted toward Florida and that thousands had moved there and more thousands wanted to and would.... [T]he very name Florida carried the message of warmth and ease and comfort. It was irresistible. "*

John Steinbeck,
Travels with Charley

Anchored in emerald waters off Islamorada
ALICIA EARLE RENNER

Quintessential Florida: a sun-kissed beach and a veil of palm at The Moorings Village, Islamorada   KEN LAFFAL

Railroad vine skims across a sandy beach at Anastasia State Recreation Area south of St. Augustine   ED KING

Saw palmettos, sabal palms, and slash pines compete for a roothold in Everglades National Park   LARRY ULRICH

Managed by The Nature Conservancy, Apalachicola Bluffs and Ravines Preserve in the Panhandle
is aptly nicknamed the Garden of Eden A. BLAKE GARDNER

A raccoon finds sanctuary at J. N. "Ding" Darling National Wildlife Refuge   WILLIAM B. FOLSOM

The pileated woodpecker is the largest of the eight
woodpecker species in Florida   JEFF FOOTT

*" All of this was still the Florida of the
conquistadores...: the unbroken
subtropics, marsh beside jungle, the bright
spread of a land burgeoning with some of
the most primitive of trees, as the palms
are. The smell was of salt and trunk rot,
and it was heady. "*

Gloria Jahoda,
The Other Florida

Jupiter Inlet Lighthouse, a pre-Civil War beacon, towers over the north bank of the Loxahatchee River   ROBB HELFRICK

The laughing gull is a common sight year-round on the Florida coast
CHICA STRACENER

The beacon at Cape Florida Lighthouse on Key Biscayne is no competition for Nature's own CHEYENNE ROUSE

Sailors take advantage of a stiff breeze as they tack around a buoy and race into the home stretch   ALICIA EARLE RENNER

The dolphin… lives with wonderful self-sufficiency in a kingdom of his own. It is a kingdom he has unselfishly invited us to share. We would be callous indeed— and what's more, foolish—not to accept his invitation.

Samuel Carter III,
The Happy Dolphins

Playful spotted dolphins in a near–dead heat
KENNAN WARD

Beguiling but carnivorous, pitcher plants await unwary insects in Apalachicola National Forest   JEFF RIPPLE

" No naturalist or genuine lover of the out-of-doors has ever been disappointed in this state. "

Helen G. Cruickshank,
Flight into Sunshine

The limpkin is known as the "crying bird"
for its loud, eerie call   JEFF FOOTT

13

Spatterdock and red maples flourish in Highlands Hammock State Park south of Sebring   LARRY ULRICH

Shell Island, a seven-mile strip of sugary sand, is a haven for shell collectors and sun worshippers alike
DONNA MCLAUGHLIN ARNOLD

A beachcomber's booty delights the eye   DONNA MCLAUGHLIN ARNOLD

Lovely Cayo Costa State Park entices beachcombers seeking solitude   A. BLAKE GARDNER

Space Shuttle *Endeavour* ignites an early dawn at Kennedy Space Center north of Cape Canaveral   RED HUBER/THE ORLANDO SENTINEL

> *From this small ancient frontier... long shining rockets have risen with incredible majesty, with unearthly detonations, wreathed in white vapor, glittering with ice crystals on their long courses above the earth, toward the moon, toward an unimaginable frontierless space, where men have already floated and stared, with their own eyes.*

Marjory Stoneman Douglas,
Florida: The Long Frontier

17

Kennedy Space Center serves up "the right stuff"
M. TIMOTHY O'KEEFE

Florida is justifiably renowned for its awe-inspiring sunrises and sunsets   LAURENCE PARENT

❝ In Florida skies, great flowers float like hyacinths on water,
burgeon, and disappear. There are misty fields of cloud, whose crops
wisp into the distance, as if you were passing so quickly that you can't
quite make out what's growing and know no more than that it may be
something to wear, soft and white and clinging to the skin.❞

Lola Haskins,
Visions of Florida

The Ho ocaust Memorial in Miami Beach, completed in 1990, was dedicated to survivor Elie Wiesel and six million other Jewish victims   JAN BUTCHOFSKY-HOUSER

The remains of Fort Jefferson nearly overwhelm Green Key in the Dry Tortugas, seventy miles west of Key West
ALICIA EARLE RENNER

❝ What of fiction could exceed in romantic interest the history of this venerable State? ❞

Edward Smith King,
The Southern States of North America

Archways to yesterdays at Fort Jefferson, which served as a prison in the 19th century   GEORGE WUERTHNER

Built by the Spanish in the 17th century and now a national monument, Castillo de San Marcos has withstood assaults by pirates and the British Navy   KEN LAFFAL

“ Wandering here, one comes to think it more than a fancy that the land itself has caught the grave and stately courtesies of the antique Spaniards. ”

Sidney Lanier,
Florida: Its Scenery, Climate, and History

Built in 1888 as a hotel, this masterpiece of Spanish Renaissance architecture
now houses Flagler College in St. Augustine   KEN LAFFAL

McKay Auditorium, now part of the University of Tampa campus, was built in 1925 to serve as a city meeting hall   MAXINE CASS

The Westcott Building, built in 1910 at Florida State University in Tallahassee, is a fine example of
Jacobian Revival architecture MAXINE CASS

The crisp skyline of Miami serves as a solid backdrop to the amorphous waters of Biscayne Bay   ROBB HELFRICK

> *The bright pastels of the buildings and the glare of the sun and the booming greenery gave [Miami] the look of a place perpetually in bloom... a backyard tropics with a touch of the Bahamas and a splash of Cuba....*

Al Burt,
Al Burt's Florida

"Bogie" makes an unexpected appearance on trendy
Ocean Drive MICHAEL VENTURA

The streamlined facades of the Art Deco District line Ocean Drive in Miami Beach MAXINE CASS

> 66 *Twenty-five years ago the Beach was tranquil, mellow. . . . Now it's an explosion of color and life. People have to take to the streets, not to walk but to dance, to wiggle their waists, their hips.* 99

Haydee Scull,
Miami: In Our Own Words

Nighttime is party time on glitzy Ocean Drive MICHAEL VENTURA

The cruise terminal at the Port of Miami from the deck of a cruise liner   DAVE G. HOUSER

Another refreshing glass of OJ in the making   WILLIAM H. ALLEN, JR.

❝ Enchantment lies in different things for each of us. For me, it is in this: to step out of the bright sunlight into the shade of orange trees; to walk under the arched canopy of their jadelike leaves… to feel the mystery of a seclusion that yet has shafts of light striking through it. ❞

Marjorie Kinnan Rawlings,
Cross Creek

Ice intentionally created by the grower helps to keep OJ OK
M. TIMOTHY O'KEEFE

Boldly advertising the local wares in Lake Wales   MAXINE CASS

Florida produces about three-fourths of the nation's oranges and grapefruit   M. TIMOTHY O'KEEFE

Beautiful but insidious, water hyacinths overrun a cypress swamp in Big Cypress National Preserve TOM TILL

The exotic blossom of the banana tree presages the fruit   KEN LAFFAL

The scarlet seed of the crab's-eye is alluring but highly poisonous   JEFF FOOTT

Morning fog tests the rapids on the Hillsborough River north of Tampa   A. BLAKE GARDNER

" How happily situated is this retired spot of earth! What an eliseum it is! "

William Bartram (1791),
Travels of William Bartram

A whitetail flaunts new antlers still cloaked in velvet
CHICA STRACENER

Rock Run Creek, replenished by a spring rain, picks its way through Torreya State Park in the Panhandle   A. BLAKE GARDNER

A pair of surprisingly graceful manatees entertains with a bit of synchronized swimming   JEFF FOOTT

" Out of the shadows they come, materializing slowly, as if beaming in from some other world. Sometimes they look like blimpy ballerinas, pirouetting in unison. With effortless figure-eights of a single flipper, they change direction. "

Jeff Brazil,
The Orlando Sentinel

Canoeists drift through placid Manatee Springs State Park
west of Gainesville   MAXINE CASS

Who knows what lurks just beneath the surface of Homosassa Springs? DOUG PERRINE/INNERSPACE VISIONS

Another day bleeds its last near Mahogany Hammock in Everglades National Park   CRAIG W. DAVIS

There are no other Everglades in the world. They are, they always have been, one of the unique regions of the earth, remote, never wholly known. Nothing anywhere else is like them: their vast glittering openness, wider than the enormous visible round of the horizon, the racing free saltness and sweetness of their massive winds, under the dazzling blue heights of space.

Marjory Stoneman Douglas,
The Everglades: River of Grass

A great blue heron on the lookout for something fishy JEFF FOOTT

The iridescent plumage of the purple gallinule is stunning and unmistakable   JEFF FOOTT

The prickly silhouette of the thornbug is a defense
against predators   CONNIE TOOPS

A snowy egret turns topsy-turvy to preen its lacy breeding plumage   HENRY H. HOLDSWORTH

Rare and secretive Florida panthers are agile in both wet and dry terrain   KENNAN WARD

Bald cypresses stand up to their knees in the Santa Fe River in O'Leno State Park north of Gainesville   JEFF RIPPLE

One can see far through the tangled thickets the gleaming water out of which rise thousands of 'cypress knees,' looking exactly like so many champagne bottles set in the current to cool.

Edward Smith King,
The Southern States of North America

Named for a mythical Greek maiden, the io moth undergoes its metamorphosis in a papery cocoon spun on the ground   NORBERT WU/MO YUNG PRODUCTIONS

The neon green anole can turn a more commonplace brown in seconds   HENRY H. HOLDSWORTH

The nocturnal Cuban treefrog is the largest treefrog in North America JOE MCDONALD

Inline skaters cruise within sight and sound of the Atlantic Ocean in Fort Lauderdale   MAXINE CASS

A toddler's quest for fun in the sun   CHEYENNE ROUSE

Tigertail Beach, at the northern end of Marco Island in the Gulf of Mexico, pampers those who long to relax   M. TIMOTHY O'KEEFE

Sand castle architect in action   ALICIA EARLE RENNER

" We are getting reconciled to a sort of tumble-down, wild, picnicky kind of life—this general happy-go-luckiness which Florida inculcates. If we painted her… she would be a brunette, dark but comely… with a sort of jolly untidiness, free, easy, and joyous. "

Harriet Beecher Stowe,
Palmetto Leaves

45

Sand and surf at Daytona Beach are always best savored at a leisurely pace MICHAEL VENTURA

The Luxurious Don Cesar Hotel presides over a stretch of beach at St. Petersburg   MAXINE CASS

The Bridge of Lions links mainlanders in St. Augustine with Anastasia Island   DONNA MCLAUGHLIN ARNOLD

Maclay State Gardens in Tallahassee brims with fragrances and hues

❝ Before you rises a scene that symbolizes the wonderful peculiarities of Florida: two capitols, in all their contrasting magnificence.... The graceful old capitol... with its peppermint awnings and graceful dome sprouting a tiny flagpole, showers you with a full sense of state history.... The modern 22-story capitol looks over its shoulder..., blocky and precise enough to have been sired by a computer.❞

Al Burt,
Al Burt's Florida

The New Capitol Building, Tallahassee's tallest structure, looms over its less intimidating predecessor DAVE G. HOUSER

Colorful Cypress Gardens, gouged from a sixteen-acre swamp during the Depression, attracts swarms of tourists to central Florida   TOM TILL

" Yearly, from the gray cities of wintry lands thousands hasten to the eternal summer of this perfumed place....."

Lafcadio Hearn,
Floridian Reveries

Flamingo incognito   M. TIMOTHY O'KEEFE

Not a whole lot bigger than some mailboxes is the nation's smallest post office in Ochopee, southeast of Naples   DENNIS FLAHERTY

It's no joke—the World's Smallest Police Station is the center of law enforcement in tiny Carrabelle
M. TIMOTHY O'KEEFE

Special delivery in Tierra Verde, a suburb of St. Petersburg   DENNIS FLAHERTY

Is it live or is it statuary, wonders a twilight visitor to Mallory Square in Key West   KEN LAFFAL

Cinderella's castle in Fantasyland sets the tone for a visit to the Magic Kingdom, one of three distinct parks in Walt Disney World   GRACE DAVIES

A monorail speeds visitors by the 180-foot-high geosphere at the heart of Epcot's Future World   M. TIMOTHY O'KEEFE

A Disney fan discovers "the wonderful thing about Tiggers"
GRACE DAVIES

> 66 *If you dò not believe in Florida magic you should not visit... Disney World, where one can ride imagination back into the delights of childhood.* 99
>
> Richard Powell,
> *Florida: A Picture Tour*

Lake Eola provides a placid contrast to the bustling skyscrapers of downtown Orlando   ROBB HELFRICK

The Universal Studios globe introduces visitors to this thrilling
theme park and working movie studio   M. TIMOTHY O'KEEFE

Musicians delight the crowds at an 1890s-style music hall on Church Street in downtown Orlando   M. TIMOTHY O'KEEFE

A gaudy welcome to Splendid China, an Orlando-area park that features detailed miniatures of Chinese landmarks   MAXINE CASS

A close encounter of the amiable kind at SeaWorld in Orlando   SEAWORLD OF FLORIDA

A flock of terns skims the sea off the south Florida coast   RICHARD GIBSON/HI-SEAS INC.

"Cheese!" says this obliging bottlenosed dolphin   JEFF FOOTT

Perhaps it is the sweet, other-worldly and quite inhuman smile always affixed to the dolphin's lips, but each time [I saw them] I felt a kind of inexplicable... tenderness toward them.... It is a feeling man has always had in the dolphin's presence.

Jack McClintock,
The St. Petersburg Times

A glimpse of Florida's most notorious resident is the highlight of many a vacation   JOE MCDONALD

> *Almost anyone who is asked to say what animal or vegetable most clearly epitomizes the color and spirit of the primeval Southeast would say the alligator.*

Archie Carr,
A Naturalist in Florida

Have jaws, will travel   ALICIA EARLE RENNER

That's close enough at Royal Palm Visitor Center, Everglades National Park   JEFF FOOTT

"Come on, folks, you can't believe everything you read!"   JEFF FOOTT

Like lacy flowers, spiderwebs punctuate the River of Grass, also known as the Everglades   LARRY ULRICH

Firm believers in a free lunch, vultures hover expectantly in the Everglades   CARR CLIFTON

Mother Nature spins her own web across a parched
stretch of the Everglades   CARR CLIFTON

❝ Nature down here is an easy, demoralized, indulgent, old grandmother, who has no particular time for any thing, and does every thing when she happens to feel like it.❞

Harriet Beecher Stowe,
Palmetto Leaves

The sago palm, a native of Indonesia, feels right at home in the company of an elephant ear plant in Orange County   STEVE MULLIGAN

" *The plant forms were too eccentric for geometry—palm, spike, spray, corkscrew, club, plume, lace, spiral. It was beautiful, but the intricacy was like the complexity of smell.* "

David Rains Wallace,
Bulow Hammock: Mind in a Forest

Commonly called deer moss, this plant is actually a type of lichen   JEFF FOOTT

A red-bloomed epiphyte, this quill-leaf air plant depends on its tree host for support, not food   TOM TILL

A boardwalk invites exploration of one of the superb beaches on Sanibel Island in the Gulf   KEN LAFFAL

The brown pelican plunges into the sea from heights of 20 to 30 feet
in pursuit of seafood   MARY ANN MCDONALD

> " *I thought I had now reached the height of all my expectations, for my voyage to the Floridas was undertaken in a great measure for the purpose of studying these lovely birds in their own beautiful islands.* "

John James Audubon,
Audubon in Florida

The roseate spoonbill scoops up small aquatic hors d'oeuvres   HENRY H. HOLDSWORTH

The dolphin fish's gymnastics and pit-bull tenacity make it highly popular with bluewater anglers   DONNA MCLAUGHLIN ARNOLD

Proud catch of the day: a six-pound bonefish   M. TIMOTHY O'KEEFE

With near-religious fanaticism, anglers try their luck from an abandoned bridge south of Marathon   ROBB HELFRICK

Great expectations in Biscayne National Park   M. TIMOTHY O'KEEFE

Commercial fishing boats nod in repose after a hard day's work on the Gulf Coast   KEN LAFFAL

" Long after the last bait is cast, tales of captured prizes or the ones that got away evoke visions of the sun, the sea and the smell of the salt air."

The Insiders' Guide to the Florida Keys & Key West

Trolling for marlin and sailfish—the calm before the storm
RICHARD GIBSON/HI-SEAS INC.

The sailfish is one of the most coveted trophy fish, but conservation-minded anglers today prefer to catch and release
RICHARD GIBSON/HI-SEAS INC.

Gearing up for underwater adventure   ALICIA EARLE RENNER

Sea oats decorate the dunes at St. Joseph Peninsula State Park, southeast of Panama City A. BLAKE GARDNER

66 The shore is an ancient world, for as long as there has been an earth and sea there has been this place of the meeting of land and water. Yet it is a world that keeps alive the sense of continuing creation and of the relentless drive of life. 99

Rachel Carson,
The Edge of the Sea

Stairway to heaven on the Gulf Coast M. TIMOTHY O'KEEFE

Waves rinse away the sand to reveal coquina rock at Washington Oaks State Gardens, north of Daytona Beach   A. BLAKE GARDNER

A mind-boggling feat of engineering, Seven Mile Bridge spans the watery gap between Marathon and the Lower Keys
DONNA MCLAUGHLIN ARNOLD

> *The Florida Keys carve their scimitar way through turquoise and amethyst and emerald and sapphire waters, and the tarpon still leap, creatures of molten silver, in the moonlight.*

Richard Powell,
Florida: A Picture Tour

Unwinding, Florida-style   DONNA MCLAUGHLIN ARNOLD

A tradition since the 1960s, merrymakers and street entertainers gather in Key West to celebrate sunset   KEN LAFFAL

Artists flock to the annual art festival on Pigeon Key
M. TIMOTHY O'KEEFE

Cuban emigres imported the art of cigar–making
ALICIA EARLE RENNER

A table for two with a view on Little Palm Island in the Keys   MICHAEL VENTURA

Sunny porches and pastel paintwork epitomize exclusive Seaside, west of Panama City   KEN LAFFAL

A row of decorative houses made to suit birds of a
different feather   DONNA MCLAUGHLIN ARNOLD

Warm and exotic Key Largo inspires Technicolor dreams   M. TIMOTHY O'KEEFE

Local color in Key West   M. TIMOTHY O'KEEFE

> " *The beach is not the place to work; to read, write or think.... Too warm, too damp, too soft for any real mental discipline or sharp flights of spirit.... One is forced against one's mind, against all tidy resolutions, back into the primeval rhythms of the seashore....* "
>
> Anne Morrow Lindbergh,
> *Gift from the Sea*

> 66 *Florida is a nice place. You ever been there? You ought to see it. Blue water, and green and lavender in the bay. Lovely at sundown. Beautiful light and air.* 99

John Ringling,
quoted in *Ringling: The Florida Years*

Kaleidoscopic hotel sign in Key Largo
M. TIMOTHY O'KEEFE

A 200-million-year-old coral reef reveals its delicate inhabitants to underwater explorers of the Keys   M. TIMOTHY O'KEEFE

A scuba diver exchanges greetings with a blue angelfish on a small reef south of Miami DOUG PERRINE/INNERSPACE VISIONS

A jewfish seems bewildered by an Unidentified
Sunken Object MASA USHIODA/INNERSPACE VISIONS

Christ of the Abyss, a memorial to perished sailors, at
John Pennekamp Coral Reef State Park M. TIMOTHY O'KEEFE

A relatively docile lemon shark and a diver eye each other warily   GARY J. ADKISON/INNERSPACE VISIONS

Nine of ten oysters swallowed in Florida are harvested, like these, in Apalachicola   KEN LAFFAL

" *Water is a presence and people live in connection with it. They fish, or deal in oysters, scallops, and shrimp. On the beach road, there are fisheries built on pilings over the water, corrugated iron oyster shacks, shrimp boats with swathes of nets.* "

Mickey Friedman,
Hurricane Season

This Marathon fisherman stalks the Florida lobster, a clawless
cousin of the Maine variety   RICHARD GIBSON/HI-SEAS INC.

Souvenir shops line the old sponge docks at Tarpon Springs, a fishing village settled by Greek seafarers   MAXINE CASS

A brass helmet tops this traditional sponge-diving suit   M. TIMOTHY O'KEEFE

The economy in Tarpon Springs is always soft   MAXINE CASS

Morning sun warms a deserted beach in Anclote Key State Preserve, north of Tarpon Springs   A. BLAKE GARDNER

Two-thirds of the endangered Key deer population, including this doe and fawn, lives in a national wildlife refuge on Big Pine Key   CLAUDINE LAABS

A leatherback turtle makes tracks for the relative safety of the surf   KENNAN WARD

Tampa, one of Florida's most energetic communities, ventures right to the edge of its namesake bay ROBB HELFRICK

> *On all these shores there are echoes of the past and future: of the flow of time, obliterating yet containing all that has gone before; of the stream of life, flowing as inexorably as any ocean current, from past to unknown future.*

Rachel Carson,
The Edge of the Sea

89

Feeding time at Busch Gardens in Tampa
M. TIMOTHY O'KEEFE

Florida boasts more golf courses than any other state, including this one at the prestigious
PGA National Resort in Palm Beach Gardens   LEN KAUFMAN

" *In Florida you won't begin to feel lonesome because you're*
the only person in your neighborhood who doesn't have a job to
go to during the day. "

George and Jane Dusenbury,
How to Retire to Florida

Is it out of the sand and into the water at Innisbrook Golf Resort in Tarpon Springs?　M. TIMOTHY O'KEEFE

Chip shot at Walt Disney World Golf Course in Orlando　M. TIMOTHY O'KEEFE

Jacksonville's forest of corporate high-rises dons a mellow purple robe at dusk   KEN LAFFAL

Million-dollar homes line Venetian Bay in Naples, southwest Florida's most sophisticated city
M. TIMOTHY O'KEEFE

The sumptuous Venetian Pool in Coral Gables was meant to disguise the scar left by developers who quarried limestone to build the city   DAVE G. HOUSER

The sun shines more on Florida than other places, promoting green subtropical abundance, the casting off of restrictive clothing, the building of swimming pools… and the overall availability of, well, warm feelings.

Patrick Carr,
Sunshine States

Bodysurfing the artificial breakers at Typhoon Lagoon in Walt Disney World   M. TIMOTHY O'KEEFE

Making a splash   ALICIA EARLE RENNER

Keeping her cool   CHEYENNE ROUSE

Key West celebrates the Fourth of July in traditionally bombastic style ALICIA EARLE RENNER

Superlatives fall short when describing Little Palm Island, a five-acre jewel that is the centerpiece of the Keys   M. TIMOTHY O'KEEFE

> *Florida has been for the American imagination not merely a geographical region but an image, a garden, Eden-like, where the striving and seeking, the rigorous pioneering and getting ahead that characterize the Land of Opportunity has been tempered and diverted by the languors of a tropical climate....*

Anne Rowe,
*The Idea of Florida in the
American Literary Imagination*

A sea kayaker weaves among the Lower Keys
MICHAEL VENTURA

Cape Florida Lighthouse, built in 1825, stands sentinel on the southern tip of Key Biscayne   TOM ALGIRE

" I hear the plaintive windsong, and I hear the soft sounds of the fan-leafs brushing against each other. It is like a litany of the land. This is the… soul of my world. "

James Billie,
quoted in
The Sabal Palm: A Native Monarch

Blowing Rocks Preserve, on Jupiter Island, provides vital habitat for sea turtles and manatees   A. BLAKE GARDNER

Autumn ignites the landscape along the Santa Fe River in River Rise State Park   JEFF RIPPLE

The waters of central Florida beg to be explored silently by canoe   M. TIMOTHY O'KEEFE

> *Here in Florida the seasons move in and out like nuns in soft clothing, making no rustle in their passing.*
>
> Marjorie Kinnan Rawlings,
> *Cross Creek*

Less agile on land than other rabbits, the marsh rabbit takes to the water when threatened   ROBB HELFRICK

An exotic bromeliad, or air plant, draws nourishment from the air and rain without injuring the tree that hosts it CARR CLIFTON

The nine-banded armadillo immigrated to Florida from Texas DOUG PERRINE/INNERSPACE VISIONS

Baton Fouge lichens emblazon cypress trunks in Loxahatchee National Wildlife Refuge   CARR CLIFTON

The Fort Myers laboratory of Thomas Edison remains just as he left it when he died in 1931—a jumble of test tubes, phials, and tripods   KEN LAFFAL

" Florida has always provided a home for individualists. . . . "

John Ames,
Speaking of Florida

Some of Ernest Hemingway's most acclaimed work was produced in this, the study of his Key West home   M. TIMOTHY O'KEEFE

The Blue Angels hang in suspended animation at the National Museum of Naval Aviation in Pensacola MAXINE CASS

Contemplating the Old Masters at the Ringling Museum of Art in Sarasota, one of the finest collections
of Baroque art in the nation   LEN KAUFMAN

The Morse Museum of American Art in Winter Park displays this and other stained-glass pieces
by the legendary Louis Comfort Tiffany   M. TIMOTHY O'KEEFE

The Everglades bask in the dawn's early light   CLAUDINE LAABS

" *For the first time I was powerfully impressed by this strange region.... This was the everglades.... Evergrass would have been truer. Far from the low margin of the creek, far as my gaze could grasp, stretched a level plain of saw grass.* "

Zane Grey,
Tales of Southern Rivers

Islamorada anglers refuse to abandon their quest for the wily bonefish   MICHAEL VENTURA

The mockingbird enriches warm, moonlit nights with amazing imitations of other songbirds   LARRY KIMBALL

Tadpoles collect in the miniature pools cupped in the leaves of a water lily   ALICIA EARLE RENNER

Water pennywort creeps across the glassy surface of Alexander Springs in Ocala National Forest   JEFF FOOTT

Tropical frangipani blossoms are reminiscent of sunset   DONNA MCLAUGHLIN ARNOLD

❝ This is the American Riviera.... a tropical paradise.... It's the Empire of the Sun. It's the Garden of Eden. ❞

character in *The Barefoot Mailman,*
by Theodore Pratt

This exotic bird-of-paradise seems poised for flight
ALICIA EARLE RENNER

The green treefrog usually gathers in choruses of several hundred, filling the night air with a cowbell-like tune   CRAIG W. DAVIS

A scarlet macaw greets visitors to the popular theme park, Busch Gardens DAVE G. HOUSER

“ *The frog Philharmonic of the Florida lakes and marshes is unendurable in its sweetness. I have lain through a long moonlit night… and listened to the murmur of minor chords until, just as I have wept over the Brahms waltz in A flat on a master's violin, I thought my heart would break with the beauty of it.* ”

Marjorie Kinnan Rawlings,
Cross Creek

"Conch houses," an unlikely fusion of Victorian, Colonial, and Tropical architecture,
are right at home in eccentric Key West   DONNA MCLAUGHLIN ARNOLD

*66 The great charm, after all, of this life, is
its outdoorness. To be able to spend your
winter out of doors, even though some days
be cold; to be able to sit with windows open;
to hear birds daily; to eat fruit from trees,
and pick flowers from hedges, all winter
long,—is about the whole of the story. 99*

Harriet Beecher Stowe,
Palmetto Leaves

The perfect perch for seekers of serenity
ALICIA EARLE RENNER

A bamboo grove at Marie Selby Botanical Gardens in Sarasota tenders a tempting
invitation to pause and reflect   ALICIA EARLE RENNER

A dream come true: sailing off into the sunset from a port in the Florida Keys   ROBB HELFRICK

" *I doubt that anyone can travel the length of the Florida Keys without having communicated to his mind a sense of the uniqueness of this land of sky and water and scattered mangrove-covered islands.* **"**

Rachel Carson,
The Edge of the Sea

An "old salt" sets a course for parts unknown
DONNA MCLAUGHLIN ARNOLD

The prow of a tall ship plows a furrow through the Atlantic DONNA MCLAUGHLIN ARNOLD

they made it possible

Florida on My Mind would have been impossible to produce without the keen eyes and technical skills of more than forty professional photographers. These women and men submitted their finest images, and the results show in this stunning collection of photos. What does not show is the work it took to get these images— the early mornings to capture the sunrise, the long hikes through swampy terrain, the endless hours of waiting for the perfect light, the hundreds of shots that didn't turn out quite right, and the high level of technical skill that was acquired through years of experience and study. To all the photographers who contributed to *Florida on My Mind,* we say thanks. We appreciate their art and their hard work.

Michael S. Sample and Bill Schneider
Publishers, Falcon

Photographers in *Florida on My Mind*

Tom Algire
William H. Allen, Jr.
Donna McLaughlin Arnold
Jan Butchofsky-Houser
Maxine Cass
Carr Clifton
Grace Davies
Craig W. Davis
Dennis Flaherty
William B. Folsom
Jeff Foott
A. Blake Gardner
Richard Gibson/Hi-Seas Inc.
Robb Helfrick
Henry H. Holdsworth
Dave G. Houser
Red Huber/*The Orlando Sentinel*
Len Kaufman
Larry Kimball
Ed King
Claudine Laabs
Ken Laffal
Joe McDonald
Mary Ann McDonald
Steve Mulligan
M. Timothy O'Keefe
Laurence Parent
Alicia Earle Renner
Jeff Ripple
Cheyenne Rouse
SeaWorld of Florida
Chica Stracener
Tom Till

Connie Toops
Larry Ulrich
Michael Ventura
Kennan Ward
Norbert Wu
George Wuerthner

Innerspace Visions
Gary J. Adkison
Doug Perrine
Masa Ushioda

For extra copies of this book please check with your local bookstore, or write Falcon, P.O. Box 1718, Helena, MT 59624 or call toll-free 1-800-582-2665
Visit our website at www.Falcon.com

Text research: JAN GODOWN
End papers: Sunrise over Florida Bay CLAUDINE LAABS
Front cover photos:
The Moorings Village, Islamorada, Florida Keys BILL SUMNER
Brown pelican MICHAEL SAMPLE

Back cover photos: Miami skyline ROBB HELFRICK
Florida panther M. TIMOTHY O'KEEFE
Quill-leaf plant TOM TILL
Unwinding Florida-style DONNA MCLAUGHLIN ARNOLD

acknowledgments

The publisher gratefully acknowledges the following sources:

Title page quote from "Time for Never-Never Land to Grow Up," by Jim Bacchus, in *Forum: The Magazine of the Florida Humanities Council*, Summer 1994.

Page 2 quote from *Travels with Charley*, by John Steinbeck. New York: Viking, 1962.

Page 7 quote from *The Other Florida*, by Gloria Jahoda. New York: Charles Scribner's Sons, 1967.

Page 11 quote from *The Happy Dolphins*, by Samuel Carter III. New York: G.P. Putnam's Sons, 1971.

Page 12 quote from *Flight into Sunshine: Bird Experiences in Florida*, by Helen G. Cruickshank. New York: The Macmillan Company, 1948.

Page 17 quote from *Florida: The Long Frontier*, by Marjory Stoneman Douglas. New York: Harper & Row, 1967.

Page 18 quote from *Visions of Florida*, by Woody Walters, with an introduction by Lola Haskins. Gainesville: University Press of Florida, 1994.

Pages 20 and 41 quotes from *The Southern States of North America*, by Edward Smith King. London: Blackie and Sons, 1875. Reprinted in *The Florida Reader: Visions of Paradise from 1530 to the Present*, ed. by Maurice O'Sullivan and Jack C. Lane. Sarasota: Pineapple Press, 1991.

Page 21 quote from *Florida: Its Scenery, Climate, and History*, by Sidney Lanier. Philadelphia: J. B. Lippincott, 1875. Reprinted by the Bicentennial Commission of Florida, 1973.

Pages 25 and 48 quotes from *Al Burt's Florida*, by Al Burt. Gainesville: University Press of Florida, 1997.

Page 26 quote from *Miami: In Our Own Words*, ed. by Nancy Ancrum and Rich Bard. Kansas City: Andrews and McMeel and *The Miami Herald*, 1995.

Pages 28, 101, and 113 quotes from *Cross Creek*, by Marjorie Kinnan Rawlings. New York: Charles Scribner's Sons, 1942.

Page 32 quote from *Travels of William Bartram*, ed. by Mark Van Doren. New York: Dover, 1928. Originally published by James & Johnson, Philadelphia, 1791.

Page 34 quote from "Manatee: The First Year of the Last Decade," by Jeff Brazil, in *The Orlando Sentinel*, Dec. 16, 1990.

Page 37 quote from *The Everglades: River of Grass*, by Marjory Stoneman Douglas. Sarasota: Pineapple Press, 1988. Originally published by Rinehart, New York, 1947.

Pages 45, 63, and 114 quotes from *Palmetto Leaves*, by Harriet Beecher Stowe. Boston: J. R. Osgood, 1873. Reprinted in *The Florida Reader: Visions of Paradise from 1530 to the Present*, ed. by Maurice O'Sullivan and Jack C. Lane. Sarasota: Pineapple Press, 1991.

Page 51 quote from "Floridian Reveries," in *Leaves from the Diary of an Impressionist*, by Lafcadio Hearn. Boston: Houghton Mifflin, 1911. Reprinted in *The Florida Reader: Visions of Paradise from 1530 to the Present*, ed. by Maurice O'Sullivan and Jack C. Lane. Sarasota: Pineapple Press, 1991.

Pages 55 and 75 quotes from *Florida: A Picture Tour*, with an introduction by Richard Powell. New York: Charles Scribner's Sons, 1972.

Page 59 quote from "How Smart Can a Dumb Beast Get?" by Jack McClintock, in *The St. Petersburg Times*, May 14, 1972.

Page 60 quote from *A Naturalist in Florida*, by Archie Carr. New Haven: Yale University Press, 1994.

Page 64 quote from *Bulow Hammock: Mind in a Forest*, by David Rains Wallace. San Francisco: Sierra Club Books, 1988.

Page 67 quote from *Audubon in Florida*, by Kathryn Hall Proby. University of Miami Press, 1974.

Page 70 quote from *The Insiders' Guide to the Florida Keys & Key West*, by Victoria Shearer and Vanessa Richards. Manteo, N.C.: Insiders' Publishing and The Florida Keys Keynoter, 1997.

Pages 72, 89, and 116 quotes from *The Edge of the Sea*, by Rachel Carson. New York: Houghton Mifflin, 1955.

Page 79 quote from *Gift from the Sea*, by Anne Morrow Lindbergh. New York: Pantheon Books, 1955.

Page 80 quote from *Ringling: The Florida Years, 1911-1936*, by David Chapin Weeks. Gainesville: University Press of Florida, 1993.

Page 84 quote from *Hurrican Season*, by Mickey Friedman. New York: E.P. Dutton, 1983.

Page 90 quote from *How to Retire to Florida*, by George and Jane Dusenbury. New York: Harper & Row, 1975. Originally published in 1947.

Page 93 quote from *Sunshine States*, by Patrick Carr. New York: Doubleday, 1990.

Page 97 quote from *The Idea of Florida in the American Literary Imagination*, by Anne Rowe. Baton Rouge: Louisiana State University Press, 1986.

Page 98 quote from *The Sabal Palm: A Native Monarch*, by Barbara Oehlbeck. Naples, Fla.: Gulfshore Press, 1997.

Page 104 quote from *Speaking of Florida*, by William L. Pohl and John Ames. Jacksonville: University of North Florida Press, 1991.

Page 108 quote from *Tales of Southern Rivers*, by Zane Grey. New York: Grosset & Dunlap, 1924.

Page 112 quote from *The Barefoot Mailman*, by Theodore Pratt. New York: Signet, 1971. Originally published by Hawthorn Books, New York, 1943.

Page 120 quote from "The In Side of Florida," by Agnes Ash, in *Venture*, February 1969.

Here's to yet another glorious day in paradise   M. TIMOTHY O'KEEFE

66 *No other part of America has the same subtropical luxuriance,*
made eternally green by soft rain, ocean tradewinds and hard sun....
It is a geographic paradise, and nearly all of its citizens or their
ancestors have come to it expecting heaven on earth. 99

Agnes Ash,
Venture